Archaeology and Ancient Cultures

UNCOVERING THE CULTURE OF ANCIENT EGYPT

By Alix Wood

PowerKiDS press.
NEW YORK

Published in 2016 by
The Rosen Publishing Group, Inc.
29 East 21st Street, New York, NY 10010

Cataloging-in-Publication Data

Wood, Alix.
Uncovering the culture of ancient Egypt / by Alix Wood.
p. cm. — (Archaeology and ancient cultures)
Includes index.
ISBN 978-1-5081-4651-3 (pbk.)
ISBN 978-1-5081-4652-0 (6-pack)
ISBN 978-1-5081-4653-7 (library binding)
1. Egypt — Civilization — To 332 B.C. — Juvenile literature. 2. Egypt — Antiquities — Juvenile literature. I. Wood, Alix. II. Title.
DT61.W66 2016
932—d23

Editor: Eloise Macgregor
Designer: Alix Wood
Consultant: Rupert Matthews

Photo Credits: Cover, 1 © Shutterstock; 2, 4, 5 top, 12, 13 bottom, 15 top, 20, 22, 23 bottom © DollarPhotoClub; 5 bottom © Jastrow/Louvre Museum; 6 top © Pitt Rivers Museum; 6 bottom, 11 top, 13 top, 18 top, 24 © Trustees of the British Museum; 7 top, 11 bottom © Manchester Museum; 7 bottom © iStock; 8 © Ricardo Liberato; 9 top © Barcex; 9 bottom © Berthold Werner; 10 top © The Petrie Museum of Egyptian Archaeology; 10 bottom © Luis Garcia/National Archaeological Museum of Spain; 15 middle © H.H. Ochmann; 15 bottom © Dreamstime; 16 © Howard Potts; 17 top © Harry Burton; 17 bottom © Jenn Arc; 18 bottom © Steve F.E. Cameron; 19 bottom © Jean-Pierre Dalbera; 21 bottom © Corbis; 23 top © Per-Olow Anderson , 25 top © National Portrait Gallery; 25 bottom © The Louvre Museum; 26, 27 bottom © A.S. Hunt; 27 top © William Casselman; 28 © Jon Bodsworth; 29 top © World Imaging; 29 bottom © Franck Goddio; all other images are in the public domain

Manufactured in the United States of America

CPSIA Compliance Information: Batch #: BW16PK For Further Information contact Rosen Publishing, New York, New York at 1-800-237-9932

CONTENTS

ANCIENT EGYPT

Archaeologists have found amazing discoveries in Egypt. The ancient Egyptians were great artists, **architects**, and craftsmen, creating some incredible buildings and beautiful treasure. Egypt is in northeast Africa. Its people lived along the banks of the Nile River. At certain times in its history, Egypt was made up of two kingdoms. Upper Egypt had its capital at Thebes. Its king wore a white crown. Lower Egypt's capital was at Herakleopolis. Its king wore a red crown. In around 3200 BCE the pharaoh of Upper Egypt conquered Lower Egypt and the country became united, with its capital at Memphis.

Upper and Lower Egypt look like they are the wrong way around. This is because the Nile River starts on the higher ground in Upper Egypt and then flows down through Lower Egypt to the sea.

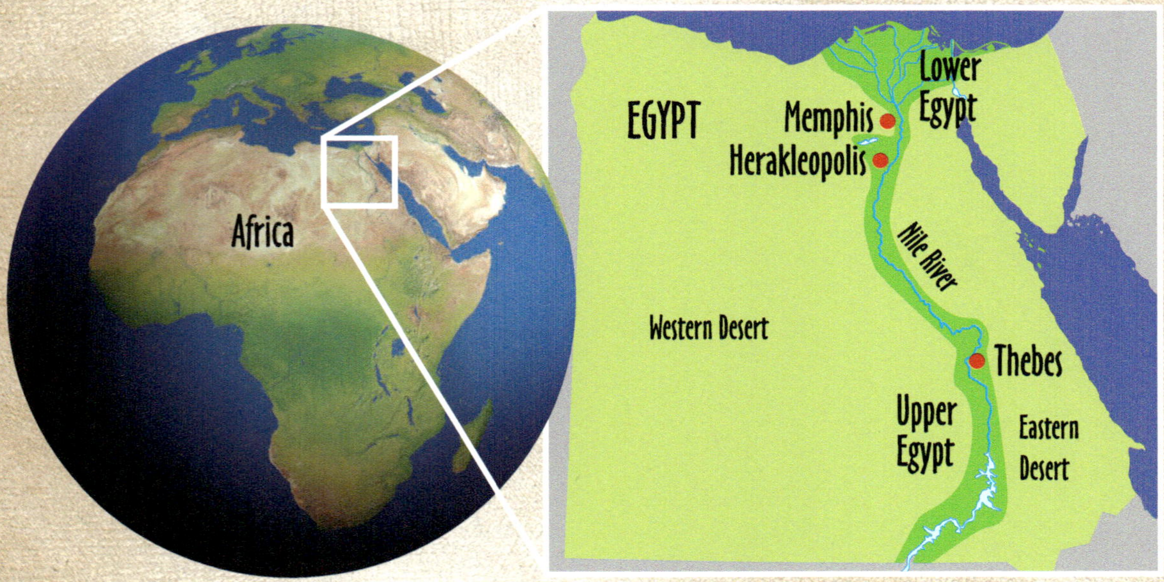

Timeline

A colored band by the page number shows each site's time period

6000-c 3100 BCE Predynastic	c 3100 - 2181 BCE Old Kingdom	2181 - 2055 BCE First Intermediate Period	2055 - 1650 BCE Middle Kingdom

The Nile River

Much of Egypt is desert and doesn't get much rain. People settled near the Nile River, where crops could grow. The river flooded each year, covering the land on either side with thick black mud. The mud was good for growing crops. Ancient Egyptians divided their territory into "red land" and "black land." The red land was the deserts, that helped protect Egypt from invaders. The black land was the land near the river where they grew their crops.

Artifact Facts

When the Upper and Lower Kingdoms of Egypt joined together, the pharaohs wore a new double crown, combining the red and white crowns of the two kingdoms.

1650 - 1550 BCE Second Intermediate Period	1550 - 1069 BCE New Kingdom	1069 - 664 BCE Third Intermediate Period	664 - 332 BCE Later Period	332 - 30 BCE Ptolemaic

GERZEH DIG

Archaeologist Gerald Wainwright and his friend Joscelyn Bushe-Fox discovered an ancient Egyptian **cemetery** at Gerzeh in 1911. Brushing away the sand at one grave they found an adult skeleton. The head had been removed and placed upright, looking west. Excited, Wainwright recognized the style of burial as from the very ancient Predynastic period!

Pottery and stone jars filled with food, drink, ointments, and oils were buried with the bodies. Several of the bodies wore beads around their waist and neck. The photograph above shows an **excavation** at the Gerzeh site. You can see the pots surrounding the curled up skeleton. The tombs date from around 3600-3100 BCE.

This mummy is from a similar grave to the one at Gerzeh, at Gebelein. The desert sand has dried out and **mummified** the body.

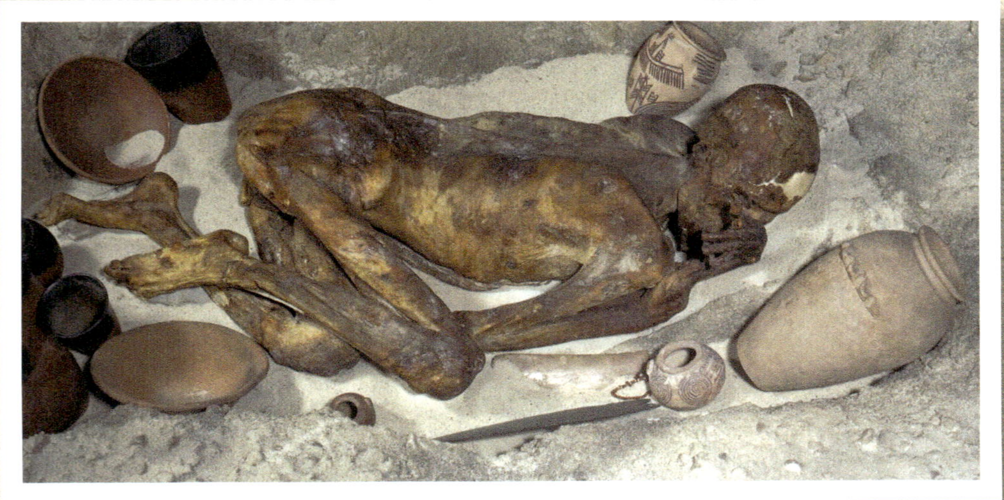

Artifact Facts

The most exciting find at Gerzeh was the discovery of several tiny, iron beads in a necklace. Why were they exciting? Because they came from a time thousands of years before people knew how to extract iron. How could they have been made so long ago?

Nine tube-shaped iron beads were found in Gerzeh. Researchers discovered that the beads also contained nickel. Nickel and iron are found in **meteorites**. Could the metal have fallen from the sky? This theory was believed until the 1980s, when experts began to think that the iron might have been produced by accident.

More recent studies are convinced that the beads were made from a meteorite. Using modern scientific equipment, scientists found that the iron had a structure that could only be found in meteorite iron. They also found evidence that the bead was made by being hammered into a thin plate and curled around into a tube. These early iron artifacts are only found in tombs of important people. Metal that falls from the sky must have been seen as a gift from the gods.

PYRAMIDS OF GIZA

The **pyramids** at Giza were built around 4,500 years ago during what is known as the Old Kingdom. When a **pharaoh** died, he expected to become a god in the **afterlife**. Pharaohs were buried in a specially built pyramid. Inside the pyramid, the tomb was filled with all the things the pharaoh would need in the next world.

The first pyramid at Giza was built for Pharaoh Khufu. His Great Pyramid is the largest in Giza. It was built using around 2.3 million enormous stone blocks. No one is sure how the ancient Egyptians were able to build them without modern machinery. Khufu's son, Pharaoh Khafre built the second pyramid. The third, smaller pyramid was for Pharaoh Menkaure. Menkaure's pyramid looks large in this photo as it is closer to the camera than the others.

The Great Sphinx of Giza was covered up to its shoulders by sand for years. It was uncovered by archaeologist Émile Baraize, in 1936.

Archaeologists made some amazing finds at Giza, including a complete boat buried in a pit! Archaeologist Kamal el-Mallakh discovered the Khufu ship at the foot of the Great Pyramid of Giza. It had lain undisturbed since Khufu's funeral. The ship was probably built for Khufu to use in the afterlife. It was one of two ships discovered at Giza. Built mostly from Lebanon cedar, it had a flat bottom, and the planks were lashed together with grasses.

Egyptian archaeologist Khamal el-Mallakh

Artifact Facts

The Khufu ship is the world's oldest intact ship, and the craftsmanship it was made with means it could sail today if it was put into the water! It has been described as one of the greatest Egyptian discoveries ever.

HERAKLEOPOLIS

After the Old Kingdom, Egypt split up again into separate states. Herakleopolis became the main city of Lower Egypt. Thebes was the main city of Upper Egypt.

In the early 1900s, archaeologist Sir Flinders Petrie excavated Herakleopolis, after fellow archaeologist Dr. Édouard Naville had left. Naville had uncovered the large Temple of Arsaphes, and then decided the area had no more remains to find. Petrie was a very organized archaeologist. He discovered another temple, early pottery, tools, and Roman remains. More recently, Spanish digs have unearthed more finds.

English **Egyptologist** Sir Flinders Petrie excavated many of the most important archaeological sites in Egypt, with his wife, Hilda Petrie.

The carving below was found by Spanish archaeologists in 1976. It decorated the wall of a tomb of a governor of Herakleopolis and his wife, and shows people bringing food as offerings to the dead.

Naville discovered the Temple of Arsaphes when he noticed an unusual dip in the land. He found six enormous red **granite** columns at the temple. Petrie had discovered written evidence that there was more than one temple at Herakleopolis. He re-excavated the site once Naville had left, and began to search. His efforts paid off. The temple he found was built by kings Senusret II and Amenemhat III long before the Temple of Arsaphes. The temple had later been rebuilt and enlarged by Ramesses II, who had reused the red granite columns that Naville had found.

Artifact Facts

Naville gave the six giant red granite columns he found to museums in the US (Boston and Philadeplhia), the United Kingdom (London, Manchester, and Bolton) and Australia (Adelaide). They are 17 ft (5.2m) tall and are now carved with images of Ramesses II.

The temple's ruined columns during the excavation by Naville

KARNAK TEMPLE

The huge Karnak Temple complex near Thebes was built over a period of many centuries. The earliest finds come from the reign of Senusret I, from the time of the Middle Kingdom. A shrine known as the White Chapel was built to commemorate Senusret I's 30 years on the throne. Compared to many of the other buildings at Karnak, the White Chapel does not look very impressive. The amazing thing about the chapel was how it was rediscovered!

The rebuilt White Chapel at the Karnak Temple

After an earthquake in the late 1800s, the French archaeologist, Henri Chevrier, discovered large pieces of carved **alabaster** stone inside a huge entrance doorway to the main temple. The stone had been used as filler to support the entrance, known as the Third Pylon. Between 1927 and 1930 all the pieces were carefully removed and reassembled to restore the beautiful White Chapel. Carvings on the walls show Senusret being crowned and embraced by the gods Amun, Horus, Min, and Ptah.

Karnak has provided archaeologists with many exciting finds. It is the largest religious site ever built, covering about 200 acres (80.9 hectares)! Karnak is home to a city of temples built over a period of 2,000 years. The Hypostyle hall is the largest room of any religious building in the world. The site also contains a vast **sacred** lake, 423 feet by 252 feet (129 by 77 m). The Pharaoh Hatshepsut had two tall **obelisks** built at the entrance to the temple. One fell, but the remaining one is the tallest surviving ancient obelisk on Earth. A great festival was held at Karnak every year. It lasted twenty-seven days. The Egyptians believed that the gods and the earth became exhausted after a **harvest** and the festival was believed to help their recovery.

Artifact Facts

This kneeling figure made of quartzite was found during excavations at the Karnak Temple site. The find dates from the Middle Kingdom.

The lake at Karnak showing two tall obelisks

PHARAOHS AND UFOs

Abydos is one of the oldest cities of ancient Egypt and one of the most important archaeological sites. Many tombs of pharaohs have been found there. In 2014 archaeologists from the Penn Museum, Pennsylvania, discovered a new cemetery containing the tombs of several pharaohs. The tomb of the pharaoh Senebkay is painted with images of goddesses. Senebkay's tomb dates from 1650 BCE.

Senebkay's body was originally mummified. Robbers had ripped the wrappings off. They were probably searching for treasure that may have been placed between the cloth strips during mummification. From studying the skeleton, experts think he was medium height and was between 40 and 50 years old when he died.

Archaeologists examining Abydos' Temple of Seti found what is known as the Abydos King List carved on a wall. This list of the pharaohs of Egypt spanned from a very early pharaoh, Menes, until Seti himself. Egyptians used a system of writing made up of pictures and symbols called **hieroglyphs**. The pharaohs' hieroglyphs are called cartouches. A cartouche is an oval with a horizontal line at one end. This shape indicates that the text enclosed is a royal name.

The magnificent Temple of Seti is built of white limestone. Started by Seti, it was completed by his son, Ramesses II.

Seti's cartouche from the Abydos King List

Artifact Facts

High on a wall in the Temple of Seti are these strange hieroglyphs. They look like a helicopter, a submarine, a glider, and a modern aircraft or spaceship! These vehicles weren't invented yet, so how did they get carved on an ancient temple wall?

TUTANKHAMUN'S TREASURE

In 1922, English archaeologist Howard Carter made a world famous discovery while working in the Valley of the Kings. He, and his team, found the tomb of the pharaoh Tutankhamun. Between the 16th and 11th century BCE, pharaohs and powerful nobles were buried at the Valley of the Kings. Over the years, more than 60 tombs have been found there. In 1922 most archaeologists thought they had found all the tombs, but Carter figured out that there was one still left — the tomb of Tutankhamun.

Artifact Facts

Tutankhamun was buried with some incredible treasure. His burial mask was made of gold and was created to look just like the young pharaoh. It covered the face of his mummified remains. Egyptians believed that this helped his spirit recognize his body in the afterlife.

Carter began excavating huts at the base of the tomb of Ramesses VI. The huts had housed the people who built Ramesses' tomb. A water boy uncovered a strange rock as he tried to make a place to set down a water jug. The sand was cleared, and revealed a step! The steps led down to what looked like the top part of a door. Excited, Carter sent for his employer, Lord Carnarvon, who had waited patiently for many years for news of a find. After Lord Carnavon and his daughter Evelyn arrived, they all entered the tomb together.

Carter made a hole in a door to one of the chambers, and pushed a candle though. The room was piled high with chairs, couches, and other goods, most of them gold! The treasure had not been seen for over 3,000 years. When Lord Carnarvon asked anxiously "Can you see anything?" Carter replied "Yes, wonderful things."

Howard Carter (kneeling) and Lord Carnarvon (standing) as they opened the burial chamber. The chamber was just as it had been when it was sealed shut. A bunch of flowers still with its petals and leaves lay by the doorway. Even the smell of perfume was still in the air!

A **reconstruction** of the treasure as it was found in Tutenkhamun's tomb

WORKERS' LIVES

Deir el-Medina is an ancient Egyptian walled village which housed the craftsmen working on the tombs in the Valley of the Kings. French archaeologist, Bernard Bruyère, and his team began to excavate the site in 1922. Archaeologists knew a good deal about pharaohs and richer members of society. This dig was interesting as it showed how the ordinary people lived. Bruyère's team discovered writings on tomb walls, **papyrus**, and on pottery, information about the everyday lives of the ordinary workers.

Artifact Facts

Many of the workers were buried in elaborate tombs when they died, too. Qeniherkhepeshef was a scribe at Deir el-Medina. He kept records of the workers' attendance. This stone **shabti** figure came from his tomb. Shabtis were servant figures that were believed to be able to serve the dead person in the afterlife.

The walled village Deir el-Medina

The village was enclosed by a wall. There were two main streets with rows of narrow houses. The houses had an entrance room, and a larger central room with a raised platform for sitting and sleeping on. The back rooms were used for storage or as bedrooms, and had a courtyard with a kitchen. Staircases led up to a roof or second floor, and down to cellars for storing pottery or valuables. There were around 70 houses within the walls. The villagers were kept apart from other people. This was for secrecy, as the craftsmen knew where the pharaohs' tombs were being built, and about the treasure that would be hidden there.

The workers in Deir el-Medina also built their own tombs. These were much smaller than the ones they built in the Valley of the Kings. The tombs were built on the mountain slopes near the village. They usually consisted of a chapel and a small underground room, sometimes with a small pyramid on top of the tomb.

In a painting from the tomb of the stonemason, Pashedu, he is pictured drinking from a stream in the shade of a date palm. Drinking water was believed to put out the fires of the **Underworld** and protect the dead from harm.

This wooden box was from the tomb of Merit, the wife of a **foreman** named Kha. The box was full of makeup, perfumes, and ointments for use in the afterlife.

QUEEN HATSHEPSUT

Queen Hatshepsut ruled Egypt for around 20 years. The male **heir** to the throne at the time was her nephew, Thutmose III. He was too young to run the country, so Hatshepsut declared herself pharaoh. Hatshepsut dressed like a pharaoh, wearing the headdress with a cobra, and even a fake beard!

One of the temple's statues of Osiris

Hatshepsut had a large **mortuary** temple built beneath cliffs at Deir el-Bahari, near the Valley of the Kings. At sunrise on the shortest day of the year the Sun shines on the rear wall of her chapel. The beam then moves right to light statues of the god Osiris, guarding the doorway. The terraces had beautiful gardens filled with exotic plants. Hatshepsut probably died from natural causes, but it is possible her nephew, Thutmose, had her killed so that he could finally become pharaoh. When archaeologists opened her **sarcophagus**, her mummy was missing!

Hatshepsut's Mortuary Temple

Egypt's chief archaeologist, Zahi Hawass, believes he has found Hatshepsut's mummy, because of a broken tooth! His team studied unidentified mummies that had been found over the years. The search narrowed to two females found by Howard Carter in a small tomb, believed to belong to servants of Hatshepsut. One mummy was in a coffin labeled as Hatshepsut's nurse. The other mummy was found lying on the floor nearby. Hawass was not convinced that this unknown mummy could be Hatshepsut, even though Egyptologist Elizabeth Thomas thought the position of her left arm over her chest suggested she was royalty. Pharaohs were usually mummified with their hands over their chests.

A box from Hatshepsut's burial chamber, inscribed with her royal seal, contained her embalmed liver, stomach, and a broken tooth. The tooth perfectly matched a missing molar in the unknown mummy. **DNA** from her bones also matched mummies from her family. Although not all Egyptologists agree, many think this proves the mummy on the floor was Hatshepsut.

Artifact Facts

Hatshepsut's mummy may have been hidden in the tomb for safekeeping because Thutmose was trying to destroy her memory. Or Thutmose may have had it dumped there!

SAVING ABU SIMBEL

On the shores of Lake Nasser at Abu Simbel, two massive rock temples are carved out of the mountainside. They were originally built during the reign of Ramesses II as a monument to himself and his queen, Nefertari. Over time, the temples became covered by sand and forgotten. In 1813, Swiss traveler Jean-Louis Burckhardt discovered a frieze from the main temple. Burckhardt told Italian explorer Giovanni Belzoni about his discovery. In 1817, Belzoni was able to enter the temples.

Legend has it that "Abu Simbel" was a young local boy who guided the men to the buried temple, which he had noticed when the sands shifted. The explorers named the discovery after him.

This smaller temple was dedicated to Nefertari. The Abu Simbel statues are the only ones discovered where a queen is the same size as the pharaoh. Usually a queen only came up to her pharaoh's knees!

Amazingly, the enormous temples at Abu Simbel were not built where they are now! The temples were moved in 1968 to avoid being covered by Lake Nasser, which was created during the building of the Aswan Dam.

A multinational team of archaeologists, engineers, and heavy equipment operators worked together to move the temples to their new location 213 feet (65 m) up the mountain. The temples were carefully cut into large blocks, lifted, and reassembled, in one of the greatest feats of archaeological engineering in history!

Artifact Facts

The exact direction that the Great Temple faces means that on October 22 and February 22 the Sun lights up all the sculptures on the back wall of the inner temple, except the statue of Ptah, god of the Underworld, who always remains in the dark.

THE CODE-BREAKER

The Rosetta Stone was named after the town where it was found. It was dug up in 1799 by French soldiers who were enlarging a fort. This block of stone is one of the most important finds in Egyptian archaeology. Written on it was the clue to breaking a code that had baffled Egyptologists for centuries, how to read Egyptian hieroglyphs!

The stone was carved in 196 BCE. It is thought to have been written by priests to honor the pharaoh, Ptolemy V. It lists all the good things the pharaoh had done for the priests and people of Egypt.

When the stone was carved there were three different types of writing used in Egypt; hieroglyphic, Demotic, and classical Greek. Many scholars could read classical Greek. As the stone shows basically the same text in all three scripts, it provided a key to understanding the hieroglyphs.

British scientist, Thomas Young (top left), and French linguist, Jean Francis Champollion (bottom left), battled to be the first to solve the secrets of the Rosetta Stone. They both could translate most of the Greek part of the stone. The puzzle was in working out which hieroglyphs matched which word or sound.

Thomas Young decided to look for names, such as Ptolemy or Cleopatra, which might be easier to spot among the hieroglyphs. Champollion figured out that oval shapes, called cartouches, contained the names of important people such as pharaohs. He also worked out that the hieroglyphs inside the cartouche represented sounds. Once he had connected the sounds to make names, he was gradually able to translate the text.

Artifact Facts

Look at this close-up of the Rosetta Stone hieroglyphs. Can you find a cartouche? Egyptian hieroglyphic could be written left to right, or top to bottom! To read them, the trick is to spot which way animals and birds faced.

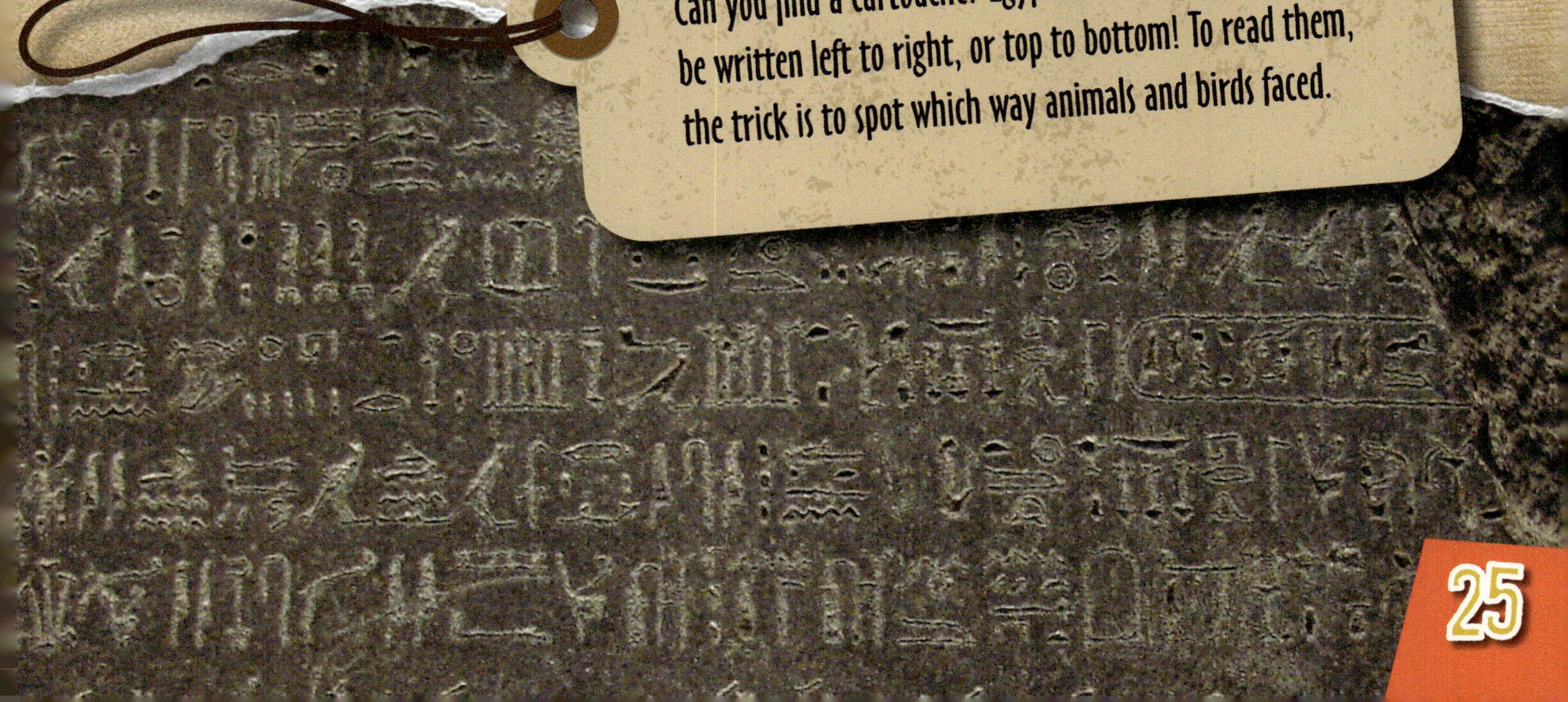

EGYPTIAN GARBAGE

A garbage dump at Oxyrhynchus is one of the most important Egyptian archaeological sites ever discovered. The site was neglected until in 1896 two young Englishmen, Bernard Grenfell and Arthur Hunt, began to explore it. They soon realized what they had found. The dry, desert climate had preserved thousands of fragments of writing on delicate papyrus.

Grenfell and Hunt were mainly interested in finding lost works of classical Greek literature. They did! They found copies of well-known masterpieces in versions closer to the original than we had ever found before.

Grenfell (left) and Hunt (right) spent every winter for ten years at the dig at Oxyrhynchus. To keep out of the heat, they spent the summer in England sorting and translating the finds.

They also found unknown works by some of the greatest authors of antiquity! Around 90 percent of the finds were ordinary documents, though, such as court records, bills, accounts, horoscopes, and private letters. All these documents were fascinating to anyone studying Ancient Egyptian civilization, too.

In their first year of digging, they found parts of several lost plays by the Greek playwright, Sophocles. They also found what appeared to be an unknown Christian gospel. Papyrus was expensive, so paper was often reused. One side may have a play written on it, and the other side may have a bill scribbled on it!

Artifact Facts

This papyrus is from Greek mathematician Euclid's work, *Elements*. Euclid wrote the work in Alexandria, Egypt, in about 300 BCE. The fragment has been dated to the end of the first century CE.

Workmen at Oxyrhynchus place their papyrus finds into a basket.

A SUNKEN CITY

Heracleion, also known as Thonis, was an ancient Egyptian city near Alexandria. Archaeologists only knew the city existed from myths and old writings. Then in 2000, after a two-year search, Franck Goddio and a team of French marine archaeologists found the ruins, under 20 to 30 feet (6 to 9 m) of water! Heracleion had sunk into the Abu Qir Bay in Egypt.

Artifact Facts

One of the most remarkable discoveries was this giant stone **stele**. The inscription says the pharaoh, Nektanebos I, wants 10 percent of taxes to go to a temple to the goddess Neith at Sais. An almost identical stele had been found at Naukratis. They are identical except in column 13, where the stele's location is named.

The divers found colossal statues, hieroglyphic tablets, and a large collection of gold coins and jewelry. Archaeologists believe that there are as many as 20,000 artifacts still on the seabed!

The old city of Alexandria was founded by Alexander the Great in 332 BCE and became an important cultural capital. It disappeared around 365 CE after a series of earthquakes and a tidal wave. In 1961, diver Kamal Abu el-Saadat persuaded the Egyptian navy to bring out a statue of the goddess Isis from harbor. Frank Goddio also dived where the pharaoh Cleopatra's palace was believed to have stood and discovered a royal pier, and a shipwreck, among other finds. Goddio said, "It's so emotional to see something that nobody has seen for 2,000 years."

This granite statue of the Osiris priest was found sunk in Alexandria's Eastern Harbor.

Divers from Goddio's team examine a giant underwater statue of a pharaoh.

GLOSSARY

afterlife An existence after death.

alabaster A white stone used for carving.

archaeologists Scientists that study past human life, fossils, monuments and tools left by ancient peoples.

architects People who design buildings.

cemetery A place where dead people are buried.

DNA A nucleic acid that carries genetic information in cells.

Egyptologists Scientists who study ancient Egyptians.

excavation A hole dug by archaeologists searching for finds.

foreman A person in charge of a group of workers.

granite A very hard rock that can be polished and is used in buildings and monuments.

harvest The gathering of a crop.

heir A person who has legal claim to a title or a throne when the person holding it dies.

hieroglyphs A character used in hieroglyphic writing.

meteorites Meteors that reach the surface of the earth.

mortuary A place where the bodies of the dead are kept until burial.

mummified To embalm and dry as or like a mummy.

obelisks Four-sided pillars that become narrower toward the top and end in a pyramid.

papyrus A material made from plants used for writing on.

pharaoh A ruler of ancient Egypt.

pyramids Structures usually with a square base and four triangular sides meeting at a point.

reconstruction Something that has been built to look like the original.

sacred Set apart in honor of someone.

sarcophagus A stone coffin.

shabti Small figures placed in ancient Egyptian tombs to serve the dead person in the afterlife

stele An upright stone slab or column decorated with figures or inscriptions.

Underworld The place of the souls of the dead.

FURTHER INFORMATION

Books

Arlon, Penelope. *Scholastic Discover More: Ancient Egypt*. New York, NY: Scholastic Reference, 2014.

Hart, George. *DK Eyewitness Books: Ancient Egypt*. London: DK Eyewitness Books, 2014.

Morley, Jacqueline. *You Wouldn't Want to Be Cursed by King Tut!: A Mysterious Death You'd Rather Avoid*. London: Franklin Watts, 2012.

Raum, Elizabeth. *Egyptian Pyramids* (Ancient Wonders). Mankato, MN: Amicus, 2014.

Due to the changing nature of Internet links, PowerKids Press has developed an online list of websites related to the subject of this book. This site is updated regularly. Please use this link to access the list:

www.powerkidslinks.com/ACC/Egypt

INDEX